Another Look

BOOKS BY HORACE GREGORY

Poetry

Chelsea Rooming House
A Wreath for Margery
No Retreat
Chorus for Survival
Poems 1930–1940

Selected Poems
Medusa in Gramercy Park
Alphabet for Joanna
Collected Poems
Another Look

Prose

Pilgrim of the Apocalypse: A Study of D. H. Lawrence
The Shield of Achilles: Essays on Beliefs in Poetry
A History of American Poetry 1900–1940 (in collaboration with Marya Zaturenska)
Amy Lowell: Portrait of the Poet in Her Time

The World of James McNeill Whistler
The Dying Gladiators and Other Essays
Dorothy Richardson: An Adventure in Self-Discovery
The House on Jefferson Street (autobiography)
Spirit of Time and Place: The Collected Essays of Horace Gregory

Translations

The Poems of Catullus
Ovid's Metamorphoses

Love Poems of Ovid

Editor

New Letters in America
The Triumph of Life: An Anthology of Devotional and Elegiac Verse
The Portable Sherwood Anderson
The Snake Lady and Other Stories of Vernon Lee
Selected Poems of Robert Browning (Rinehart Editions)
Evangeline and Other Poems by Henry Wadsworth Longfellow

Selected Poems of E.E. Cummings
The Mentor Book of Religious Verse (in collaboration with Marya Zaturenska)
The Crystal Cabinet: An Invitation to Poetry (in collaboration with Marya Zaturenska)
The Silver Swan: Poems of Romance and Mystery (in collaboration with Marya Zaturenska)
Selected Poems of George Gordon, Lord Byron

ANOTHER LOOK

POEMS
BY
HORACE
GREGORY

HOLT, RINEHART AND WINSTON

New York

Published simultaneously in Canada by Holt, Rinehart and Winston of Canada, Limited.

Library of Congress Cataloging in Publication Data

Gregory, Horace, 1898–
Another look.

I. Title
PS3513.R558A8   811'.5'2   75–29791
ISBN 0–03–015396–4

First Edition

Book design by Mary M. Ahern
Printed in the United States of America
10 9 8 7 6 5 4 3 2 1

FOR

MARGARET ROCKWELL

AND

HENRY LEROY FINCH

". . . whose philosophic eyes
Look thro', and trust the Ruler with his Skies,
To him commit the hour, the day, the year,
And view this dreadful All without a fear."

—The Sixth Epistle of the First
Book, from *Imitations of Horace*,
by Alexander Pope

Acknowledgments

I am deeply grateful to the editors of the following publications, *Modern Poetry Studies*, *The Nation*, *New Letters*, *The New Yorker*, *Poetry* (Chicago), *Poetry in Crystal* (Steuben Glass—The Spiral Press), *The Quarterly Review of Literature*, and *The Salt Creek Reader*, for printing some of the poems in this book. In preparing this manuscript, I am indebted to the critical advice of Joanna Zeigler, Marya Zaturenska, and Patrick Bolton Gregory.

TABLE OF CONTENTS

Another Look

The Moonlit Curtains
Stir at Three O'Clock

Ancient Colloquies

. . . & Testament

Another Look

ANOTHER LOOK

Gentlemen, the arts!
                    Some scrawled on canvas,
Some fired in glass, steel, iron, copper—
Tons of material, montages to oblivion
Slowly sinking through museum floors—
The pull of earth is very strong.

And these are relics of our century,
Souvenirs of Kronos from the Netherworld,
Roots clinging to them, wild vines and grasses.

And yet, precariously tilted toward the sun,
There is a mirage, while from its vapors
Mycenae's Lion Gate lifts to the sky,
Cloak-wrapped and wary, a Spartan Warrior
Still stares at us.

Erect and easy, relieved of roof and cornice,
A pair of Maillol's wandering Caryatids
Step out of shadow, and in a shower of light
There is Brancusi's pale, ethereal
Torso of a Young Girl.

As the mirage blurs, as if a leaf were torn
From *The Book of Kells*, there is a glimpse
Of a rain-shouldered Celtic Cross—

Caught up and held in a moment of grace,
These vanish out of time, then reappear—
They belong to the Fates,
And are of a source and power
Neither of earth, sea, sky—

They are beyond the arts.

The Muse Behind the Laurel

She talked twelve hours straight, sunset till morning,
waves soaring up the walls, against the ceiling:
"That was a moth escaped from your right hand;
it is a Goddess," she cried, "or a near-Goddess,
wings beating down the dark, unceasing night.
Make me imperishable and violent, all wings,
a Muse of History: blood, hail, and fire
still falling from the skies—

                    see, I am broken,
a thankless prophetess, held in a bulletproof cage
for fools to stare at."

                  Was that her fate?
And was she fit for sanatorium or museum?
Not quite.

        O she was artful,
but not a work of art.

           Both hated and loved,
she was far too fragile to be a saint,
certainly too precious, perhaps too human,
too much of this world—

               thin silks and jewels,
ruby and onyx, still swept through her mind,
would probably drown her.

                Yet she was always
beautifully rare.

She is behind us now,
                   behind clipped laurel
in the rear garden above the well-deep pool,
eyes to the ground:
                 she is indifferent
to her image in the water.
Her ways are virginal, sleepwalking empathy
pouring to heaven on a summer night.

She will not threaten you, nor sing, nor weep.
And should you question her, she may not hear you,
and if you gaze at her, she will not turn,
and if you touch her, she is as stern as iron—
an effigy of peace, and painted white.

A LEDGE OF ROCK

                leaning through fog,
a tempting foothold
                far above earth,
while far below it,
                the dangerous, death-devouring sea—
Napoleon saw it
                at Saint Helena,
fixed in his telescope.
Spring, Summer, Winter,
                the Classical Seasons sway
in flux around us
                where the Furies walk,
blood in their footsteps;
                by a trick
of the tongue
                in hope to blind the Evil Eye,
they are also "The Benign Ones,"
arriving with gifts,
                looking like flushed
and pretty girls
                around a Maypole.
There they are
                as though their being were
inevitable Nature,
                the track, the way

of mountains, valleys, and rich plateaus,
larkspur, honeysuckle,
                    violets and lilies,
dying and flowering,
                    breaking through
hoar-frost and thaw,
December melting in the breath of Spring.
And far above us,
                    as though leaning through air,
the glistening ledge of rock,
under the unfolding,
                    opening rays of the sun.

Seven a.m. in Cold Blue Air

The White-Haired People
                    train their binoculars
On wintry trees,
                    on scarlet tanagers against the snow,
On flickering sparrows,
                    on vagrant starlings
(which Audubon said
                    were "good to eat"),
On hawks and jays.

The White-Haired People do not own guns.
They are extremely quiet;
                    they are noiseless-footed;
They grip binoculars
                    now tight, now tighter,
Swiveling up and down
                    now close, then closer
Into Companionship
                    of sky and wing,
Into Friendships
                    of claw and feather—
Intimacies of nest and burrow—
                    then on again,
Following
                    The Trail of Squirrels.

Though peaceful
          and very discreet,
The Way is dangerous.
                    Yet binoculars
Are always secure, intact.
                         Their lenses are
Indomitable.
          They never fail to possess the trees,
The creatures within them,
                              the entire terrain;
A faulty strategy
             might lead to wars.

The White-Haired People
                    are alert and brave.
Their gaunt binoculars
                    sweep out
To the uttermost branches
                         of leaning trees
Above the glassy rocks
                    of the Abyss.

Off Capri

Beyond the rocks, the beach—
a flash of water:
white foam, and where it turns, the sea-green fires.
Was that a hand,
raised head, and a white shoulder?
Was that a dolphin in the broken wave,
the ancient white, night-rider of the sea,

or deep-sea lioness who turns her side
in flaming spray
against the falling sun?
Life within life is there,
and disappears
to deeper reach of seas beneath far waters
to wake, to rise again as fair Dione,
Mother of Venus, earliest of mermaids:

her glittering arms held high,
her white hands braiding
the sea anemone in green-gold hair,
her eyes the fire of jewels against the sunset—

a careless bathing quean:
men drown with her;
she is no mistress for the wary sailor:

she smiles, he turns,
then feels himself afraid—
only a god could take her in those waters,
herself a goddess for a mortal moment
before the waters close above her head.

Elegy and Flame

It stepped into my room:
A deep, yet luminous shadow clung to the wall,
Steadied itself, then came up taller,
And took on character.
                         It turned its head,
Smiled, bent over me:
Portly, red-cheeked, benign.
                         It was Dudley Fitts:
" 'From Carthage I have come—'
All in quotation marks," he said,
"By God, I am a pedant. I always 'pull
For Prime.'
          Do you hear bells ringing?
When I read aloud
                Death of Patrokles,
ILIAD, Book XVI,
                    I made a schoolboy football-captain
                    weep!
O Helios-Achilles, thy brightness over me!
And with Meleager of Gadara
                    I walked with Heliodora:
Petals in her hair: white violets, narcissi,
Myrtle, and chiming lilies,
Innocent crocus, dark, clever hyacinths,
Roses, heavy with dew—
                Heliodora, Heliodora."

Behind his voice, there were strains of music:
Vivaldi at Evensong.
                    And above the altar,
Dudley at the keys.
                 Beyond the transept,
Gold shafts of light,
                    then increasing darkness,
And his voice again,
                  "Being a thimbleful of ashes
Among the shades,
                   I have enjoyed a loss of earth.
I have come a long way
               after Death."

SIEGE AT STONY POINT

Three Voices Speaking

Birds, birds—birds, birds, birds—
A darkening of wings across the sky,
A half a million birds dropped from the air
Flying through sleep, through half-lit dawns and hours,
Black Myrmidons in passage everywhere,
Starlings and crows, ferocious wrens,
Voracious hawks, and vultures drinking oil
Empty our lamps while foraging rooks
Deplete our fruits and strip the willows bare.

Some say, "The birds are sent by Eskimos,
From antique Crees in Arctic wildernesses,
From stark Siberia, or Greenland's glassy waters,
From dark-skinned countries, fast in endless cold."
Others insist they sailed from County Clare
Straight up from fallen cottages, wrecked iron,
Moss-ridden stones, and broken angels
Lying among dank stubble and the thorn.
And ravens, fifty thousand strong and heady,
Are among the lot, their red eyes glaring.

Aristophanes once knew the birds as brothers,
He half implied this transient universe

Was theirs to wander, cherish, or remake—
The voluble Hoopoe, or raging parakeet—
But what of Earth?
                              that strange, elusive,
Far distant apparition of orange light,
Seen from a cockpit on the rim of outer space?
The gods may well desert it.
It is there for anyone to take.

The Moonlit Curtains Stir
at Three O'Clock

THE MOONLIT CURTAINS STIR
AT THREE O'CLOCK

The silences of old men signify:
1) Closed doors that lead upstairs
To empty attics—or
2) Premonitions of death-rattle
In the skull—or
3) A rising wave of self-
Consoling pity—or
4) An epiphany of wisdom in a closet—
Or, at last,
The sphinxlike joy
Of supernatural quiet.

* * *

"A poem is . . ."
Dear friends, you are too portentous—
Step out of my moonlight!
In poetry, as in true love
(For Venus is a revengeful mistress),
The unpromised, wordless ecstasy
Is almost perfect.

* * *

Men select fruit carefully:
                    quince-green,

Russet, orange, sallow:

                           they test its virtue

With calipers and paring knife.

And yet, how often The Tree of Knowledge

Is mistaken for The Tree of Life.

DETOUR IN JANUARY

At the site of the house D. W. Griffith filmed in
Birth of a Nation. Here it is viewed from the road
between it and the waters of an abandoned canal.

Willows at Piermont are moonlit girls
Trailing white arms and glimmering hair
Across the stream.
                Where the mist wavers
Great columns stand—Palladio redux—
A giant doll-house with an open door:
The fan-light's broken, mold in its crevices,
Watercress and moss,
A signboard at the gate: "No thoroughfare."
Neighbors declare
                the place is treacherous—
The Winter Wraith lives here, her breath in vapors—
Yet tonight is warm
As barefoot Echo walks through halls and chambers;
She is deranged and lost while her Narcissus
Is safe beneath the flux of the canal,
Disheveled, glancing shadows everywhere.

As we turn away
                the willows bend and quiver

In January thaw:
> there is a smell of earth—
A premonition of the thrust of Aries.
Daemon and spirit
Who awake unwary seasons of the year.

"Peace in Our Time"

Invaders have leaped ashore,   teeth gleaming:
Docile, obsequious   hands and shoulders—
Bodies dark with hair   and forearms black:
Fresh coffee served   among our Doric ruins.
We had invited them   to attend our wants,
To be brisk and silent—   to fight our wars,
Appease our wives—   to guard our gates,
Prepare bed-chambers,   to man the ships,
To mount watch-towers: "Present arms. Halt!"

On battlefields we raise   triumphal arches,
And sign peace treaties.   The sunlight over us,
The days are lovely: Laburnam swaying
Its golden head,   Jasmine in flower,
And among the grasses,   Larkspur and Lilies—
Suburban quiet   where we choose to walk.

Yet at night we hear   continual echoes
From unlikely places: the bleating of Sheep,
The gallop of Zebras,   a Jaguar screaming,
And behind the arras   incessant whisperings:
One might well imagine   all our cities
Have gone up in flames.   We lie awake.

To the Last Wedding Guest

"Here is my precious cake,"
Cried the wide blue-eyed,
Won and captured, smiling bride,
"With napkin, knife, and plate:
It is here to eat
As your eyes glide
Between the folds of my white veils—"
Silks, satins flowing
Among quick limbs in whiteness held,
Nearness in white.

"Eat of my cake
Brought by the caterer in white,
Cake in a glass bell, flowered,
Snow-crystalled, starred
In silver light
On cloth and plate."

"Eat of my secret,"
She might well have said,
For it is there
Among the secrets of the wedding night—
All that is white-limbed, young, and fair
Shall know its sign:
As the white rose flushes with a drop of blood,

So is this secret spread.
The gifts bestowed in white
Turn as a prism turns
Within the waiting eye
Of faces greeting
The downward-stepping, ever-descending stair:
See how the groom gleams
In a golden spiral
As the bride's gaze, steering slowly in his light,
Shall find her body within his arms,
There to be caught and held as all joys are,
Wordless in the brief silence after prayer,
Held in the blue-reflected summer sky
Before the coming of a darkening wind,
Before the waking of increasing storms.

As the cake is cut
For guests to eat,
Look how the bridal wreath
Leans over earth,
The tremulous, shaken
Bough, leaf, and flower
Piercing the hour
Of bell-chiming fragrance within a summer night,
Each leaf and bough
To reappear
Through seventy winters of deepening ice and snow.

The lacquered car, the floating bridal suite,
Rests at the embrace
Of the wedding-night hotel.
The belated wedding guest who had missed the bride
Stands in the hall
As though he had seen the reflection of her face,
Heard lips that say, "Or early guest or late,
Eat of my cake. It is my life.
It is why you came.
It is my gift to everyone,
Even to the last fragment on a covered plate."

THE SMOLDERING LIGHT

"Whistler lighted a single candle. . . . Turning a
canvas that faced the wall, he examined it
carefully . . . with the candle held near it. . . .
There was something tragic, almost frightening,
as I stood and waited, in watching Whistler; he
looked suddenly old, as he held the candle with
trembling hands, and stared at his work, while
our shapes threw restless, fantastic shadows, all
around us."
    William Rothenstein in his *Men and Memories*

Night stirred around him. He held the candle
high above his head.
These were his canvases he said:
"My Symphonies, Concertos, Adagios,
my life: yellow and ochre, the sun in air;
then silver and blue, swept in a trail of smoke
across the harbor—
            the script is there:
my life approaches
            a condition of music."
Over here's a frightened girl,
half-naked in tulle, a spray of maiden-fern
between her thighs. Ineffable whiteness
in her very presence.

"No, no! She is not Persephone,
not ravished, but spared.
I believe she vanished into a denser forest
than the whispering Underworld itself—a trembling quiet
entering the deepest green."
The hot wax scorched his hand.
                                    "Look," he went on,
"at the smallest canvas: a blaze of gold, flames
reflecting flames, and, at the center,
a knot of fire, and, behind the fire,
an opening rose."
                    He seemed almost drunk—
then he straightened up:
                            he caught his balance.
"All these are very wonderful," he said,
"but each imperfect—
all errors of the hand, the mind, the heart—
I move beyond them to a sightless fall of sky
that meets stilled waters."
                            He let the candle drop.

Ancient Colloquies

AN ANCIENT COLLOQUY:
THE QUARREL

"You can't put me out of the house—"
"O yes I can."
"You can't put me out of the house—"
"O yes I can."
"You can't put me out of the house
As if I were
A mosquito or louse—"
"O yes I can."

"You can't push me off the earth—"
"O yes I can."
"You can't push me off the earth—"
"O yes I can."
"You can't push me off the earth;
You can't cut off my breath
Where I have cried
And wept since birth;
"You can't push me off the earth—"
"O yes I can."

"You can't throw me out of the world—"
"O yes I can."
"You can't throw me out of the world—"
"O yes I can."

"You can't throw me out of the world
Where everything
Is bought or sold,
Where empty youth
Grows cracked and old,
Where everything
Is bent and swirled—
You can't throw me out of the world."
"O yes I can."

ONE ABOUT ONE: ONE SPEAKS

"Here is my friend,
His to assume
That all I am
Is his to share:
He wears the very color
Of my hair,
My hat, my stick:
And if I walk,
He follows me;
He imitates my pace,
And, if willfully,
I turn about-face,
He faces me.
He is like
A standing mirror
Down the hall:
He stares my stare;
No, he will not strike
Me; he's my dear friend;
He will not break
The mirror;
He is here
On a friendly call.
He wears my hat, my stick,
And swaying slightly,

He is my fiend—
Daemon and quick—
Of course, my friend.

"He wears my lips, my smile:
Look at his profile!
It is my forehead,
My round blue eye,
My nose, my chin;
He tilts my hat,
He swings my stick—
Is this not
Great flattery?
He has no choice
But to use my voice;
I hear it floating
Upward to the sky.

"Meanwhile my friend
Takes off my hat,
Leans on my stick,
Agile and politic
As I could never be
To everyone, to the entire
Applauding company
As if he were

My own best enemy—
Remarkably uncontrite,
Astute, polite,
Extremely courteous,
Discreet, yet generous,
Generous as a flower
Exhaling its perfume
In a sun-lit room.

"Suddenly
He walks away—
He seems to find
True fitness in my skin—
O he has little guilt,
No sense of sin—
While down the hall
He wears
My self-same smile:
He is trying to explain
Again, again
My faults, my flaws
Which he forgives
(O he is saintly,
The living model
Of forgivingness).

"He waves at me,
Then cheerfully
Steps up to me
Through the open door;
He takes me by the hand.
His friendship has the power
To endure
Beyond all things,
Even beyond the universe,
Even beyond the end
Of hope and joy:
He is here to stay,
So he insists
He is my friend."

"FULL FATHOM FIVE"

                    the lodestone wavers . . .
There you may read *The Ages of Man*
Etched in quicksilver
                    on a granite wall
At the bottommost level of the China Sea
In beams of light
                    the great round eyes of sharks
Go journeying there
                    through cave and portal,
Drift by and fall away, then reappear:
"At the stroke of ten,
Man is an animal,
At twenty a lunatic,
At thirty a failure,
At forty a fraud,
At fifty a criminal,"
At sixty he is the living ghost
Of all his being,
                    smiling and affable,
He takes your hand, he grips your arm,
Eager to tell, and tell again
How fate had made him
                    animal, lunatic,
Failure, fraud, and evident criminal—

There, in the glistening waters,
He stands before you.

He has begun to talk:
He ignores the traveling monsters of the sea.

DEATH & EMPEDOCLES

Glittering, adroit, the Sicilian wonder
Stepped from the sea, spoke to the crowds:
"I was first a girl, then a blundering boy,
Then a briery bush (Ankh into Crucifix!),
Then a bird, a fish: and last of all,
Your friend, Empedocles.

                        I come to greet you."
Scattered applause, then groans and hisses:
A woman's voice: "He was my lover.
He taught my hands to conquer snakes."
And other voices: "Take him away. His face
Has the look of death."

                "The distant west
Turns green, then violet. There are tremors
In the earth and menstrual heat. People are warned:
There are ashes falling."

                Some saw him leap
Deep into Aetna:

                a roar of smoke, slow lava pouring—
(We found his sandal near the crater's lip)—
Smell of psychosis, metempsychosis in the air:
Earth and its caverns towering over him;
His way was lost in flames, a Mandrake forest—
He could not unkindle fire, unwind the spell:
He was neither Herakles nor Ganymede,

While madness (the hope of fame) walked at his side.
The night seeped everywhere, the waters dark.
Streets had turned treacherous, and crowds fell quiet—
Each waiting for a comet in the sky.

EPICTETUS & OTHER STRANGERS

A middle-aged Roman native speaks to a friend:

"Handsome as Poseidon, white-haired as winter,
Here's Epictetus limping through the gate.
He is dressed in rags, for like all Stoics,
He delights in poverty—
Which is the rich man's effort
To out-trick the evil eye,
To out-wit the Fates.

"And there are crowds behind him,
Students and women, eager for discontent,
Strayed wives and secretaries
Who wander here like visitors from Thrace
To talk of miracles, to dream, to gossip
Of 'Dangling Orpheus
Whose severed head, still hot with blood, went singing
Undying magic down blind, hurtling waters . . .'
Do you believe them?"
                              "No."

"As for Eurydice, the truth is this:
That girl was all too happy to escape
Back to her little room, her Netherworld
To take deep pleasures from her Lord of Night.

"Now turn to Epictetus, chronic wonder,
Ageless, perhaps,
Death cannot throw him, he is much too supple,
Too muscular, too quick.
                    O he is clever!
And if we listen to his stories
We are like children come to watch the sunset.
We hear him saying,
                    'Do you see that cloud,
A thread of lightning through it,
Less than a vapor fading against the sky?
That vapor is the image of my spirit,
My very breath that vanishes in air.
And should I disappear,
                    it is my being
Set free at last to rise with Hesperus
Above those glimmering islands in the west.'

"Do you find him arrogant?
                    Then so do I.

"The man is dangerous,
                    even his whispers
Haunt the increasing dark,
And in this twilight, tower, street, and city
Fall into nothingness.
                    I cannot rest."

PLESSIS-DU-PARC-LES-TOURS

(After Paul Murray Kendall's *Louis XI*)

Louis XI at fifty-nine, high in his gallery,
Looked ancient, thin as parchment, lighter than air.
And above his hat, a tumult of wings:
Osprey and parakeet and rich jeweled bat,
Rubies for eyes set in brown velvet:
"Rare, rare," cried his eager merchants, "fine and rare!"

"Rare," said the King, "while poor white
Indolent Truth lies drowning in her Well.
Gaze at my tapestries: that flying snake
Escaped from the Tree of Eden—
That salamander from the lips of Hell—
All rare, extremely rare!

"Below, beyond us is the hithering Loire,
Our broken mirror of the night and day,
Steering as if forever through summer pastures,
Sunlight and meadow in a haze of years.
And at my side, what of these frail wonders?
A Sicilian donkey!
                        A Barbary wolf,
Coy as a marmoset, has fallen asleep
Between my knees.

And over here,
Frost-coated reindeer from the snows of Sweden—
God knows they're rare."
                              The King leaned down
To stroke a greyhound bitch,
To tell her Death was near, was closing round them
Where Nothingness walks into Nothingness,
A Shadow passing into vanishing Shade.

"And now," said Louis, "excellently rare
Is this, my effigy in gilded copper,
Myself a rough-clad, wakeful, long-haired boy
Kneeling in homage to Our Lady of Cléry."

The Sentimental Lover:
On the Burning of Corrina's Hair

(After Ovid)

How many times I said, "Stop pouring
Those vicious silver bleaches on your hair.
No need to dye it now—it hangs in ribbons!"

(Lovely Corrina is a perfect goose:
Her natural hair was gloriously rich:
It fell below
Her waist, her hips, and her sweet thighs.)

Darling, your hair was delicate to touch;
One feared to braid it—it was as fine as silk,
Finer than silks that little girls from Asia
Wear at a feast—
And fragile as the spider's glittering thread,
Its colors drifting neither to black nor gold,
But were of that pure light
That breaks through wandering shadows cast at noon
And through the bark-stripped cedars on the hill.

Yet at each moment of a summer's day,
It was never quite the same:
It fell a hundred ways, in waves, in ripples—

Nor did a comb's tooth tear it—
Docile it was, and bright, and never angry.
(Servants who dressed Corrina's hair could never
Quarrel with it—it was too gentle—
Nor did Corrina—in a wild temper—
Strike at the girls. She was as genial
As her joyful hair—
As when I see her yield to love each morning,
Languid and naked,
Serene as sunlight on her blessed bed,
Her hair in charmed disorder
Across one shoulder—
                              and she as tempting
As an escaped Bacchante down from Thrace
Fallen at ease within a green-wrapped forest.)

We must return to her poor, helpless locks of hair,
So soft, as innocent as new-grown feathers—
What trials, what terrors
Their souls endured in heated forks and pliers!
Why twist, why torture them with coals and fire?
O iron-minded girl, take pity on them—
They were not made for the deceptive arts—
A wind-blown disarray was half their charm.
And these scorched fragments, torn and burnt,
Were once your dowry by the grace of Venus:
They made blythe Bacchus and Apollo jealous.

(One day I had a vision of Dione—
And O her wave-washed tresses
Swayed with the motion of her jeweled sea-waters,
And they were artless as Corrina's hair—
Dione caught up in the arms of Jove.)

My Dear, no more of brooding
                              on your ill-fated hair.
I saw your mirror drop to the floor.
You had been frightened
By the stranger's face within it.
(Even now, I see her face, flushed and unhappy,
As she tries to hide her tears
Behind frail hands—while there, across her knees,
There, like a parcel,
Sent to the wrong address,
Lie the charred tresses that were once her treasure.)

My Dear, the curse was your own foolishness,
A girlish vanity to court the world's opinion—
Yet even I know hubris
Rides our desires—
Pride is our ruin—and too much modesty
Insults our Maker—while too much talk
Fades in the wind . . .
                        Come, let us kiss,
And with your arms around me,

You are no less loved, no less enchanting,
No less beautiful—
Only the wordless gift uplifts the heart.

A miracle, my Love, is sure to happen:
No, not tomorrow, nor the next day after—
But in the swift, unceasing metamorphosis
That sways our lives and rules the Zodiac,
Early one morning, the world will stop to say,
"Look at Corrina—
Has anyone else on earth such marvelous hair!"

. . . & Testament

. . . & Testament

In the lines below the voice heard is that of John
Gregory (1783–1880), one-time mathematician at
Trinity College, Dublin, who during the 1850s
was a prospector and civil engineer in the pioneer
settlement of Wisconsin. In 1853 he published a
book, *Resources of Wisconsin*, distributed in
Ireland, and so written as to guide the Irish to
America. As he speaks, one may imagine his
wraithlike presence holds the book in its right
hand.

Exiled from Dublin and the Celtic Cross
in darkest sleep, the trembling night between us,
alone I mount the stairs at Trinity
to chart the stars that sway with Liffey's tide
and wake tomorrow on the Irish Sea. . . .

I have lived my life (that shadow in a mirror!),
whiskey and hope in air, then deeper drinking,
hat lifted gallantly, then left, then right,
to placate unpaid bills, old promises,
to ward off Time, guilt hidden in the clock,
to step aside from gray-haired enmities,
mislaid appointments at lost streetcorners.

Turn me face up—and I was King of Hearts,
and of a kindred where each man I met
was once a gentleman, or half a gentleman,
or Lord Lieutenant, or half a scoundrel neat—

There was the hour when I saw Robert Emmet
lean from a crowd to wave his hand at me,
He lit a candle in the firmament,
a strong wind blowing:
O when my nation takes its place
among the ruins of the earth . . .
                                    Do I misquote him?
Almost, but for the better.
                           He could outface
his waiting destiny around the corner,
and so could I.
The night came under a cold moon when he died.
                                    Limerick, 1848

There was my patron, the shrewd Monteagle,
and at his house, the Duke of Devonshire
who kept me talking into dawn, both smiling
at what I wished to be—
myself, bankrupt schoolmaster in a storm.
                                    Och, they
would make me, if they could, Astronomer Royal
to sit at ease in Cassiopeia's Chair
to watch the seasons drift, brief spring to winter,

hunger at harvest while famine eats the crop . . .
And "would you teach the naked where to go,
the innocent Irish to unheard-of places,"
away from Dublin with its black-bird towers,
its violet twilights in October doorways?

Behind me I saw starving generations
treading each other down to nothingness,
their turbulent, weeping souls in Purgatory—
and could I rescue them, even the dying?
I was ingenuous, and never orthodox—
O God, forgive me for my foolish pride!
The Castle gates fell shut . . . Good-bye, my city.

Milwaukee, 1880

Here, where Wisconsin maples climb the sky,
return to Calvary where grass-hedged flowers
open their stars till noon, witness my grave,
assemble seasons, count the days, the hours
fallen into rubble—dust the many years.
And in this crevice, thigh-bones and skull,
white souvenirs of skill and hope
closed in a room where love and wit expire
scarcely a shadow of my soul remains.

And from this universe, a last escape?
I should have made an empire of this land

of golden savages and careless waters,
fresh dells and hills,
                        pine-cloistered winter forests,
and through calm summers, orchards and dales . . .
I saw my shining Monticellos fade
into weird lakes and climbing wildernesses
capricious as my memory for names.

Now, my estate:
I, John Gregory, Esquire, ninety-six,
strayed resident of time and stellar space,
being aware of the uncertainties, deceits
and sleepless terrors of the human lot,
being of sound mind (God help us!), wide awake,
of curious, labyrinthine memories,
do hereby make aloud, publish, declare
a last will to the winds, a testament
voiding all previous wills and codicils,
hopes, wishes, and despairs,
                        hereby bequeath
my genius to the dubious universe.
Item: I leave behind me
clapboard and iron, rooted in river clay
to be given away, the earth well lost;
my sons inherit
ten square miles of storm and rain.

EARLY APRIL MORNING

This is the day that I began.
                    This is new year's
in the terse calendar that opens with my name:
April and south winds in the sky repeat the same
rhythm, and the indigenous body hears
spring at morning waking the same trees that always
bear the sun on slender branches that somehow rise
out of dark streets down-circling nightward
                              and our eyes
turn from roots gathered and unwinding
                         under doors and hallways.

It is not the season, but the inevitable
return of seasons that unshapes the days, the hours
caught in the mind, and builds them new again:
                              flowers
and grass covering a ruined city.
                    From wild Aquarius
into waiting Aries, I retrace the day my breath
first issued toward my last decade:
let choir, spire, earth, O Trinity, answer death.

ABOUT THE AUTHOR

Horace Gregory's *Collected Poems* won the Bollingen Prize in 1965. He has also received the Loines Award from the National Institute of Arts and Letters and the Fellowship Award from the Academy of American Poets for his "distinguished contribution to American Literature." Among his adaptations from Latin verse are *The Poems of Catullus* and *The Metamorphoses of Ovid*. Of his *Collected Poems*, Theodore Weiss in *Poetry* (Chicago) wrote, praising ". . . its passionate detachment . . . this in the midst . . . of stone-making terror, the shield's art that, as it contains the gorgon, highlights it with lucid, human seeing."

Horace Gregory is married to Marya Zaturenska, who received the Pulitzer Prize for her second book of poems. They live in an eighteenth-century cottage at Palisades, New York.